Jack London

A LIFE OF ADVENTURE

Jack London

A LIFE OF ADVENTURE

by Rae Bains
illustrated by Wayne Geehan

Troll Associates

**Howell
Southeast School
Media Center**

Library of Congress Cataloging-in-Publication Data

Bains, Rae.
 Jack London: a life of adventure / by Rae Bains; illustrated by
Wayne Geehan.
  p.   cm.
 Summary: A biography of the American novelist and short story
writer who sought and wrote about adventure.
  ISBN 0-8167-2513-6 (lib. bdg.)   ISBN 0-8167-2514-4 (pbk.)
  1. London, Jack, 1876-1916—Biography—Juvenile literature.
2. Authors, American—20th century—Biography—Juvenile literature.
3. Adventure and adventurers—United States—Biography—Juvenile
literature. [1. London, Jack, 1876-1916. 2. Authors, American.
3. Adventure and adventurers.] I. Geehan, Wayne, ill. II. Title.
PS3523.046Z58 1992
813'.52—dc20
 [B]   91-3927

Jack London

A LIFE OF ADVENTURE

The muscular young man stood at the railing of the steamship *Umatilla*. Below him, deckhands rushed around, loading supplies for the long voyage north. It was June, 1897. Gold had been discovered in the Yukon. Word spread instantly and the great gold rush was on. Thousands of men and women, dreaming of huge fortunes, came to San Francisco by train, by wagon, by sea, and on foot. They were in a frenzy to reach the riches waiting in the frozen wilderness of northern Canada.

Jack London, the twenty-one-year-old man at the ship's railing, was impatient for the *Umatilla* to sail. He knew nothing about the bleak, icy, windswept world up north. But that didn't scare him a bit. London wanted to find gold. And there was something even stronger that drew him. He had a need to pit himself against the harsh cruelty of the northern wasteland. For Jack London, life itself was an endless adventure.

John Griffith London was born in San Francisco on January 12, 1876. His stepfather's name was also John London, so the boy was called Jack from the day he was born. Flora and John London, Jack's parents, were poor. They always had grand ideas of getting rich, but they didn't know how to make their ideas work. One failure followed another.

Mr. London tried being a farmer, a carpenter, a sewing-machine salesman, a sheriff, a prison guard, and a shopkeeper. Mrs. London tried to be a spiritualist, someone who claimed to have contact with ghosts. She gave piano lessons. She ran a boarding house. She worked with her husband on the farm and in their grocery store. The Londons never gave up trying.

Jack's parents were so busy, they had little time for him. The little boy was often left in the care of his stepsister, Eliza. Eliza and another sister, Ida, were Mr. London's daughters from an earlier marriage. Eliza was eight years older than Jack. But she was more than a big sister; she took care of Jack and Ida as if she were their mother.

When Eliza was in school, Jack had another baby sitter. She was Jennie Prentiss, a neighbor with two children of her own. Jennie gave Jack a great deal of love and attention. And Jack loved her very much.

Some days, Jennie wasn't around, and little Jack was left alone. He never forgot how that hurt. When he was grown up, he described the feeling as a hunger. But this hunger wasn't for food. Jack was starved for love.

From the time he was eight months old until he was four, Jack's family lived in Oakland, just across the bay from San Francisco. In 1880, the Londons moved to a twenty-acre farm in Alameda, California. Now there was nobody to look after Jack during the day. So twelve-year-old Eliza took him to school with her.

Jack had to be very quiet while the classes went on. He sat on a box in a corner of the room and looked at pictures in books. He tried to read the words so he could learn what the books said. At home, Jack begged Eliza and Ida to teach him to read. They wanted to help him but they didn't have the time to help him. Homework and household chores left no time for their little brother.

One evening Mrs. London was mending socks when she heard Jack pretending to read aloud from a book.

"What are you doing?" she asked him.

"Making up a story to go with the pictures," Jack answered.

"Would you like to learn to read the words that are really there?"

"Oh, yes, Mama! Please!"

Mrs. London smiled, put aside the mending, and sat Jack on her lap. The reading lessons began right away. Mrs. London was very happy that Jack wanted to learn. "You are a clever boy," she told him. "You must make the most of that. We don't have a lot of money, so you have to use your wits to carry you to success. Have faith in yourself, no matter what!"

Jack London faced many hard times as a child and as a grownup. There were days when every meal—breakfast, lunch, and dinner—was potatoes, and nothing else. There were months when the only clothes he owned were those on his back. But no matter how bad things got, Jack never forgot what his mother said. She believed in him, and that made him believe in himself.

When Jack was five years old he started going
to school. He loved everything about school.
Reading and writing were great fun, and so was
playing with the other boys and girls. Jack wanted
to stay in Alameda forever.

But the farm was doing so well that the Londons
decided to buy a bigger place. They sold the farm
and bought a seventy-five acre ranch near San
Mateo, California.

The ranch was on the coast of the Pacific Ocean. The land was rugged and bare. Day after day fog rolled in, blanketing the countryside in damp, gray gloom. There were no playmates for Jack. Eliza spent all day doing housework. Ida was working in a laundry in a nearby town. Mr. and Mrs. London were busy running the ranch. Once again, Jack was all alone.

The six-year-old's new school was in the town of Colma, California. It was a long walk from the ranch to the one-room schoolhouse. The school was an unhappy place, and Jack wished he did not have to go there. The teacher did not know how to control the class and he was mean to the children.

Jack hated the Colma school, but he still loved to read and learn. He had a way of escaping unhappiness—through books. For him, books were like doors that opened to happier worlds.

One afternoon, as he walked home from school, Jack found a book on the road near his house. It was a novel called *Signa,* by a writer named Ouida. *Signa* was the story of a poor Italian peasant boy who grows up to be a rich and famous violinist and composer. It was the first book Jack ever owned.

Jack read the book again and again, and dreamed of his own great future. Because the last forty pages of the book were missing, he never knew how the book ended. But that didn't matter to Jack. He made up a different ending each time he read *Signa*. As Jack London wrote many years later, this book was the star he hitched his wagon to when he was a child.

Three other books were important to Jack London. One was a collection of African adventures by a French writer named Paul du Chaillu. Another was the life story of U.S. President James A. Garfield, called *From Canal Boy to President.* The third was *The Alhambra,* a book of stories by the American writer, Washington Irving. This was Jack's favorite book when he was eight years old.

Jack read his precious books over and over. He promised himself that one day he would have adventures and travel everywhere, just like the heroes in his books. He imagined himself going off to sea in a great sailing vessel. In his mind he felt the sea spray, the rush of the wind against his face, and heard that wind whistle through the ship's rigging.

Jack pictured himself meeting strange, wonderful people in distant lands. He dreamed of finding buried treasure, and of taming a wilderness. Young Jack wrote the thrilling stories in his head. Each story had his hero facing terrible dangers and always coming out on top.

In 1885, the Londons moved again. This time it was to an eighty-seven-acre ranch in Livermore, California. The family owned olive trees, a vineyard, fruit orchards, and a few horses. But to Jack, the Livermore ranch was just one more place to be lonely and poor. In some ways it was even worse than the other places the Londons had called home. Ida had already gone away to work. Now Eliza left to get married and live in another town. There was nobody to talk to, and twice as many chores for Jack to do.

When Jack was ten years old, the family moved back to Oakland. They had lost everything, including the ranch, and they were almost broke. The Londons rented an old house in the city and lived in two of its eight rooms. They rented the other six rooms to boarders. Mrs. London did the cooking and cleaning. Mr. London took a day job in a vegetable market, and a second job as a night watchman.

For the next three years, Jack went to school in Oakland. He got good grades in English, bad ones in math, and he barely passed his other subjects. The school was in a rough neighborhood, and many of the students were tough street kids. Jack didn't like to fight but he was able to defend himself if he had to. He didn't have to very often. He was strong and looked sure of himself. That was usually enough to keep the bullies away.

Even as a boy, Jack worked hard. Every morning and evening he delivered newspapers. The three dollars he earned each month helped pay family expenses. Jack also made a little pocket money by working on an ice wagon.

In those days, there were no refrigerators. People kept food from spoiling by storing it in iceboxes. The icebox was a wooden cabinet with a metal section inside for the ice. In hot weather, ice was delivered every day. In cool weather, deliveries were made every other day. Jack helped the ice-cart driver cut the ice into large blocks for delivery to the customers. It was back-breaking work.

Jack also worked as a pinsetter in a bowling alley. Today, pins are set in place by machines, but when Jack was a boy, bowling pins were set by hand. The pinsetter kept out of the way while the bowler threw the ball. After the bowler finished his turn, the pinsetter quickly replaced the pins on their marks. It was noisy, dirty, and dangerous work. Pinsetters sometimes got hit by a flying pin or a bowling ball.

Jack didn't have many free hours. Still, he found time every day to read. He borrowed two books a week from the Oakland Public Library. As he wrote many years later, "From my ninth year, with the exception of the hours spent at school... my life has been one of toil.... Of course, I continued to read. Was never without a book."

When Jack was thirteen, he left school. The family was in debt, and the teenager needed to earn a living. He went to work in a fish cannery, slaving over a machine for ten cents an hour. He worked six days a week, with only Sunday for rest.

Some days, Jack worked twelve to sixteen hours straight. Once, during a busy period, he was at his machine for thirty-six hours, with time off only for quick meals. None of the other employees worked as hard or as long as Jack. He worked in the cannery the way he did everything—with all his strength and heart. Some months, Jack was able to bring home as much as fifty dollars. He gave every penny he earned to his mother.

There was just one thing the thirteen-year-old wanted for himself. One day Jack saw a small boat at a dock near his home. It was old and needed repairs, but Jack set his heart on owning it.

"Will you sell her?" he asked the owner.

The man nodded. "Eight dollars and the skiff is yours," he said.

Jack grinned. "I don't have the money now," he said, "but I can earn it. Please don't let anyone else have her."

To get the money for the skiff, Jack did extra work on Sundays. He scrubbed decks, furled sails for yachtsmen, swept the floors of offices and stores, and collected and sold scrap to junk yards.

It took Jack two years to save the eight dollars. Then he bought the boat and quit his job. He had a plan. He was going to make money sailing the waters of San Francisco Bay. As skipper of his own boat, Jack went into the fishing business. He sold the fish and oysters he caught to peddlers and seafood canneries. The work was exhausting. At the end of each day the fifteen-year-old was bone-tired, but happy. He was his own boss!

In a good month, Jack earned as much at fishing as he had at the cannery. But sometimes his fishnets were empty. Sometimes there were only a few oysters in his traps. So, to make a few dollars more, Jack joined the Fish Patrol. The Fish Patrol was like a seagoing posse. Its job was to stop oyster pirates from stealing shellfish from the traps of honest fisherman.

Oyster pirates sneaked out after sunset. They raided the oyster traps and used the darkness to make their escape. But the Fish Patrol was more than a match for the pirates. The patrol's boats sat silently in coves, just out of sight. As soon as the pirates started to haul the traps aboard, the patrol boats pounced. In moments they had the pirates under arrest.

Working in the Fish Patrol was dangerous. The pirates often used fists and knives against the lawmen. Whenever a fight broke out, Jack was right there alongside his fellow officers. He was young, but he quickly earned the respect of the older sailors and fishermen.

Jack was sure he could earn more money in the fishing trade if he had a larger boat. Then Jack saw just what he wanted. It was the *Razzle Dazzle*, a tall-masted sloop. Its owner, a man called French Frank, wanted three hundred dollars for it. None of Jack's family had that much money and no bank would lend three hundred dollars to a teenage boy like Jack.

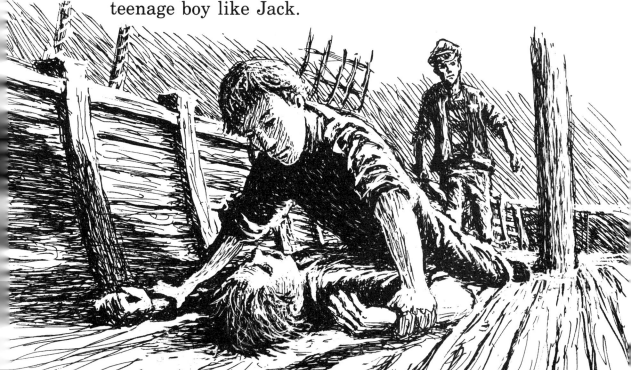

So Jack went to Jennie Prentiss. She was a sensible woman who had worked hard and saved some money. When Jack explained why he needed the three hundred dollars, she willingly said yes. Like Jack's mother, Mrs. Prentiss had faith in the teenager. Jack promised to pay back the loan, and that was good enough for her.

Even though he worked hard, Jack London did not make a success of his fishing business. It cost more than he expected to make the *Razzle Dazzle* seaworthy. Jack had to pay sixty-five dollars for a new mainsail. He had to pay his assistant's wages, even when the catch was poor. Money also went for new nets, traps, bait, and supplies. Jack was never able to make a profit.

Then something happened that crushed his dream. While he was away from the boat one night, a gang of bay pirates raided the *Razzle Dazzle.* As London later wrote, "They stole everything, even the anchors; and later on, when I recovered the drifting hulk, I sold it for twenty dollars. I slipped back the one rung I had climbed, and never again did I attempt the business ladder."

It took years for Jack to repay Jennie's loan. But she got every penny of the three hundred dollars. And when Jack London was a famous, wealthy writer, Jennie Prentiss lived in his house and helped to care for his two small daughters.

In the winter of 1893, seventeen-year-old Jack decided to go to sea. He signed on for a year as a deckhand aboard the *Sophie Sutherland*. The ship was a three-masted schooner, a sailing vessel that hunted seals in the North Pacific. It was a rough year but it taught Jack a lot. "With my own hands I had done my trick at the wheel," he wrote, "and guided a hundred tons of wood and iron through a few million tons of wind and waves....I am aware of a pride in myself that is mine, and mine alone."

Soon after he returned home, Jack read that a newspaper, the San Francisco *Morning Call,* was holding a writing competition for young authors. Jack jumped at the chance to put his sailing experiences into words. He worked feverishly, writing and rewriting until he was satisfied. He finished the article just before the deadline.

Jack's mother took the ferry across San Francisco Bay and hand-delivered the article to the newspaper, just in time. But it was worth the effort. Jack's exciting tale of adventure won the twenty-five dollar first prize. As thrilled as he was by the money, Jack was even more excited at seeing his words and name printed in the newspaper.

Jack was sure he could earn a living at writing, but he was not able to sell any of his stories and poems. Times were hard, so Jack went to work in a jute mill, making burlap. After that, he shoveled coal into the furnaces of an electrical company's engine room. The steady paycheck was a good thing, but it didn't satisfy Jack. He was still itching for adventure.

In the spring of 1894, Jack left home again. For the next two years he lived the life of a vagabond. He traveled all over America, going wherever chance took him. He rode on wagons down dusty country roads. He rattled across the land in railroad boxcars. He hiked for miles, from town to town, city to city. He met all kinds of people.

Jack learned how to avoid being caught by the railroad detectives who searched boxcars. He learned how to get along on his wits and his muscles. He took odd jobs to earn money for food. Sometimes he stood on bread lines, or went from house to house, asking for a meal in return for doing chores. Some nights were spent in hobo camps, where Jack listened to the stories told around the campfires.

In Buffalo, New York, Jack was arrested for vagrancy. A vagrant is a person with no legal address, no job, and no money. Vagrants in Jack's time were kicked out of town or thrown into jail. Jack was given a thirty-day jail sentence.

The month behind bars was a nightmare. Jack was surrounded by hot-tempered, hardened criminals. He lived every day in fear. The guards treated the prisoners like animals, and the prisoners treated each other the same way.

As soon as he got out, Jack made his way back home to Oakland. There was only one thing he wanted now—to be able to write stories for everybody to read. But Jack needed more education. He had quit school so early, there was a great deal he did not know about many subjects—things a writer should know.

With the same drive that helped him to succeed as a boy in a man's world, Jack dived into his studies. He earned A's and B's in all his subjects and completed high school in one year. At the same time, he worked as a janitor in the school buildings. He also wrote ten short stories for the high-school magazine.

Then Jack decided to go to college. To be admitted, he had to know algebra, physics, foreign languages, and other advanced subjects. So he went on an almost-impossible crash course of self-instruction—and passed the entrance examination! Jack enrolled at the University of California at Berkeley in the fall of 1896.

Berkeley was a wonderful place to learn, but the young man felt out of place. All his classmates had lived quiet, uneventful lives, while Jack had already done things that they had only read about. The other students didn't understand Jack or his inner needs.

Jack wrote all the time—stories, poetry, essays, humorous pieces—pouring his ideas onto page after page. Then, one day, he told his mother he was leaving school. She begged her son to finish college, but his mind was made up. He was going to be a writer now, and that was all there was to it.

For the next three months, Jack worked in a laundry and wrote in every spare moment. But again, he sold none of his writing. Then came July, 1897, and his adventurous trip to the gold fields of the Klondike.

When Jack returned to California a year later, he had $4.50 in gold dust, and a fortune in memories. His mind was bursting with the world up north. It was a world of hunters, miners, trappers, saloon keepers, sled dogs, wolves, bears, Eskimos, icy river rapids, avalanches, fights, the beauty and fury of winter, the bravery and madness of fortune hunters. It was a world that was waiting to be revealed in his words.

Jack London immediately set to work writing his stories. And this time his efforts paid off. In 1900, his first book, *The Son of the Wolf,* was published. It was an enormous success. The book made the Yukon real to millions of readers, and it made Jack world-famous. He went on to write fifty books and many stories and essays in the next sixteen years. And he continued to live a life of adventure. He worked as a war correspondent; lived in the slums of London, England; sailed to the South Pacific....Most of all, Jack wrote about everything he saw and did.

By the time Jack London died at the age of forty, he had crammed a dozen lifetimes into one. More than any other writer, he helped shape the images of the Klondike that remain to this day. The world that exists in *The Son of the Wolf, The Call of the Wild,* and *White Fang* is a world that will live for as long as people read and seek adventure.